CONTENTS

By Toshie Takahama

SHUFUNOTOMO CO., LTD.

Tokyo, Japan

Mobile of Pigeon
(Hanging Ornament)

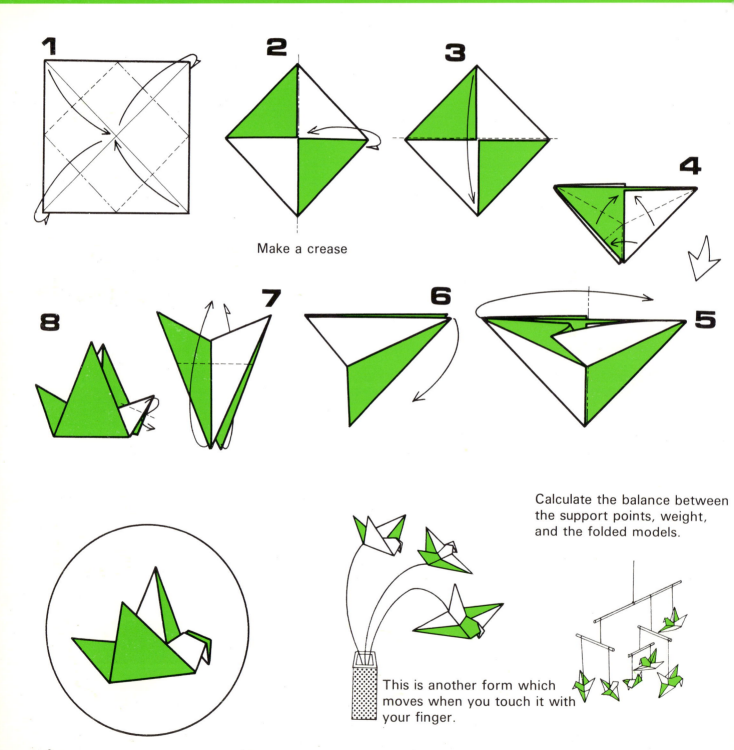

2 Make a crease

Calculate the balance between the support points, weight, and the folded models.

This is another form which moves when you touch it with your finger.

Fancy Ball
(Hanging Ornament)
Variation of Mrs. Molly Kahn's Tree Ornament

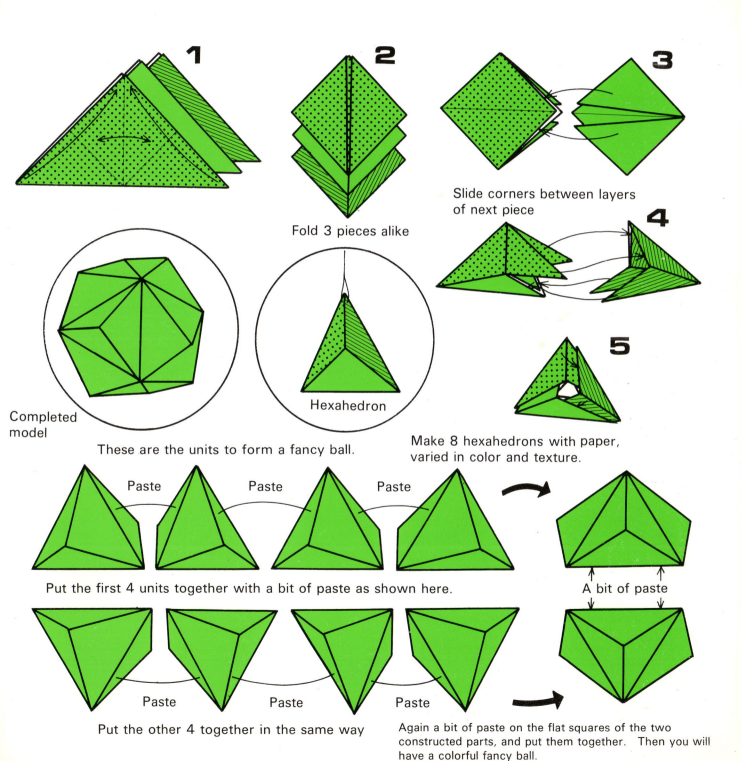

1

2

Fold 3 pieces alike

3

Slide corners between layers of next piece

4

Completed model

Hexahedron

These are the units to form a fancy ball.

5

Make 8 hexahedrons with paper, varied in color and texture.

Paste   Paste   Paste

Put the first 4 units together with a bit of paste as shown here.

A bit of paste

Paste   Paste   Paste

Put the other 4 together in the same way

Again a bit of paste on the flat squares of the two constructed parts, and put them together. Then you will have a colorful fancy ball.

Peacock
(Room Accessory)

Fold in along the marked lines

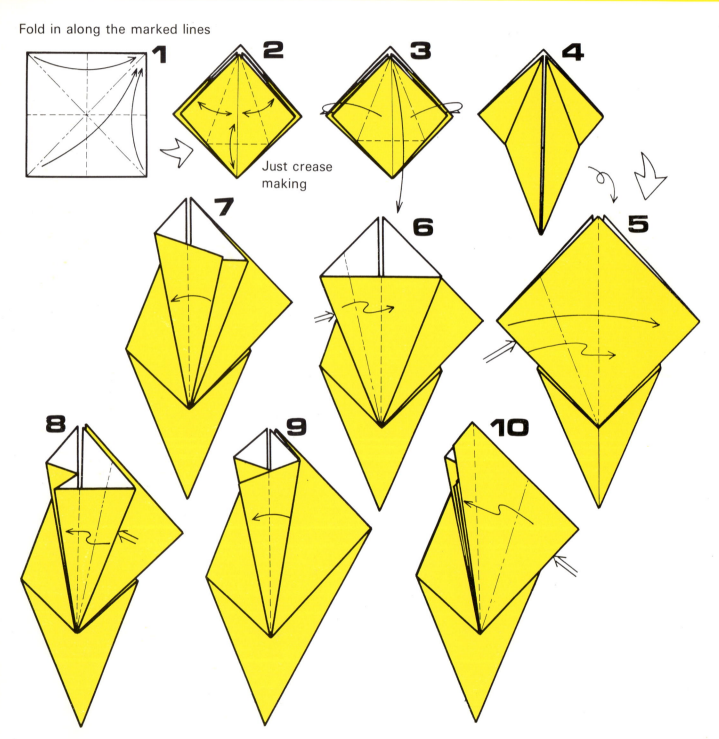

1

2

Just crease making

3

4

5

6

7

8

9

10

11

12

13

14

15

Reverse
Fold II

16

Reverse
Fold I

19

17

Reverse
Fold I

18

Beak

Reverse
Fold II

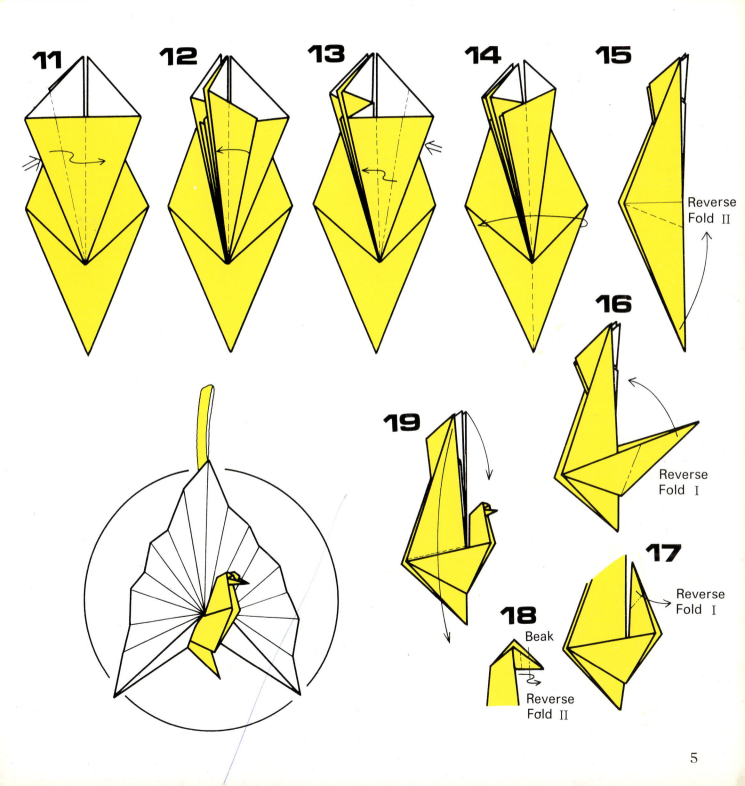

Owl
(Room Accessory)

BIRD BASE (1—5)

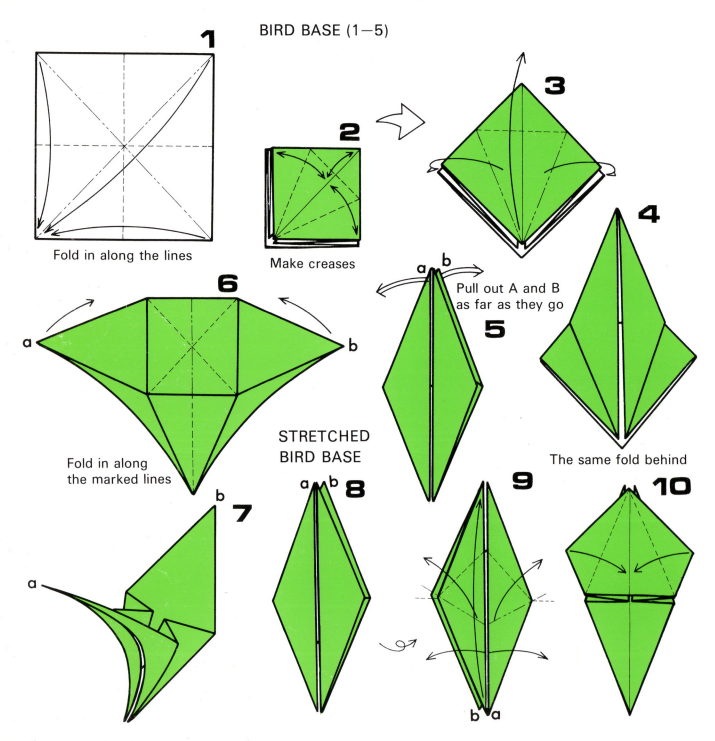

1 Fold in along the lines

2 Make creases

3

4 The same fold behind

a b Pull out A and B as far as they go **5**

STRETCHED BIRD BASE

6 Fold in along the marked lines

7 a b

8 a b

9 b a

10

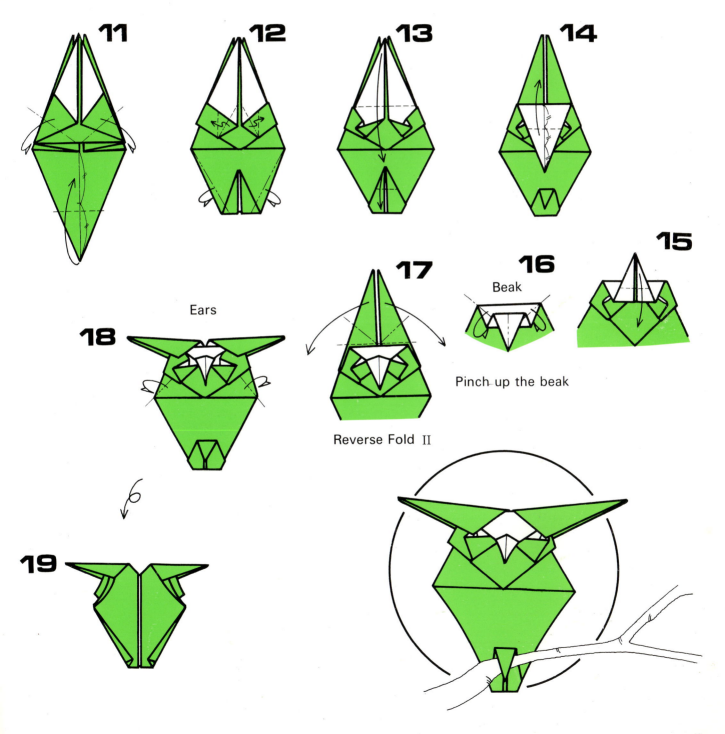

11

12

13

14

15

16

Beak

Pinch up the beak

17

Reverse Fold II

Ears

18

19

Butterfly
(Room Accessory)
From Mrs. Mitsue Aoki's Swallow-tail

WATERBOMB BASE

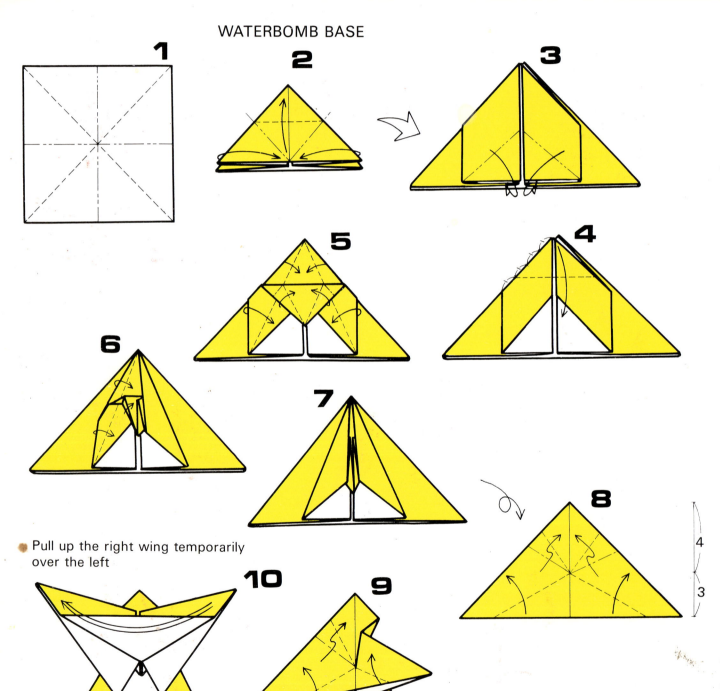

Pull up the right wing temporarily over the left

Fold in along the marked lines

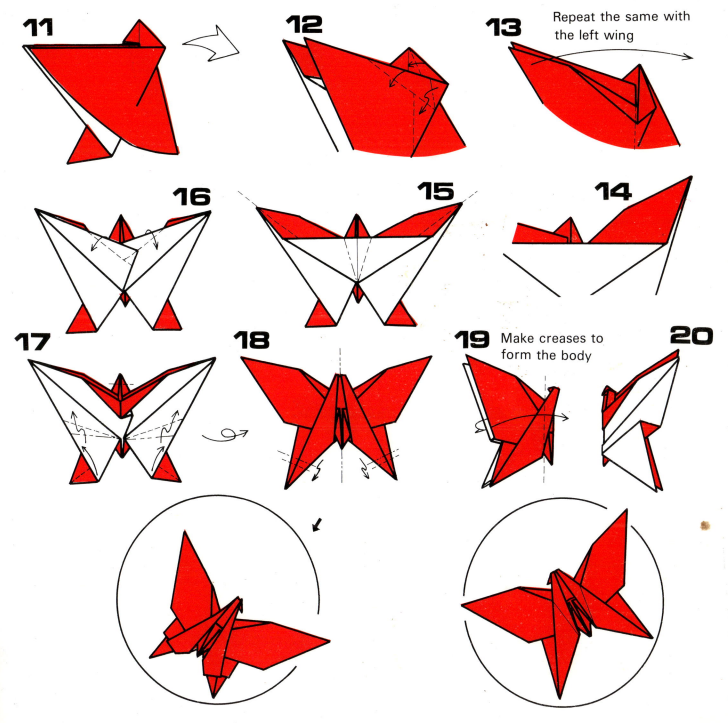

11

12

13 Repeat the same with the left wing

14

15

16

17

18

19 Make creases to form the body

20

Elephant
(Container Ornament)

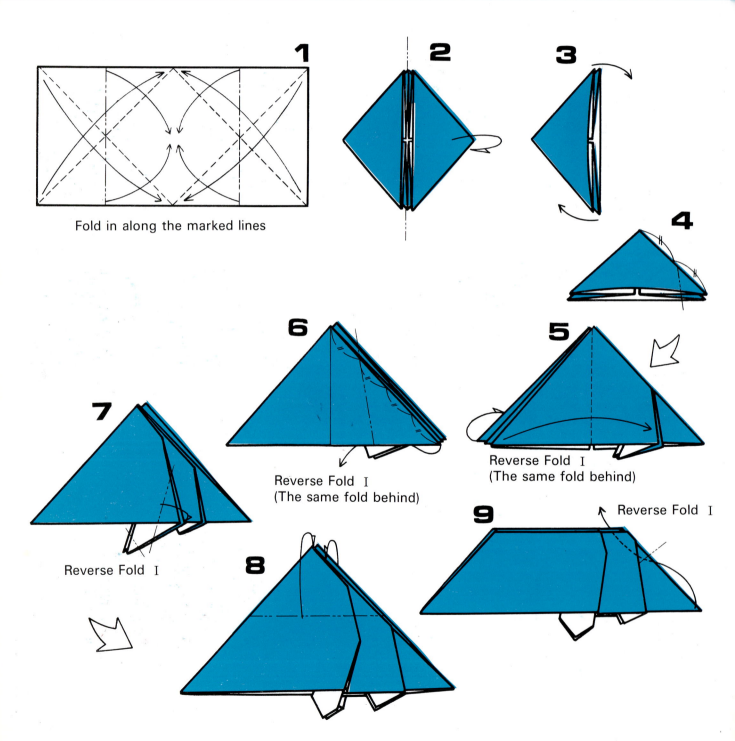

1

Fold in along the marked lines

2

3

4

6

Reverse Fold Ⅰ
(The same fold behind)

5

Reverse Fold Ⅰ
(The same fold behind)

7

Reverse Fold Ⅰ

8

9

Reverse Fold Ⅰ

10

Tail

11

Inside of the tail

12

13

Reverse Fold I

15

14

16

Head

17

Reverse Fold I

18

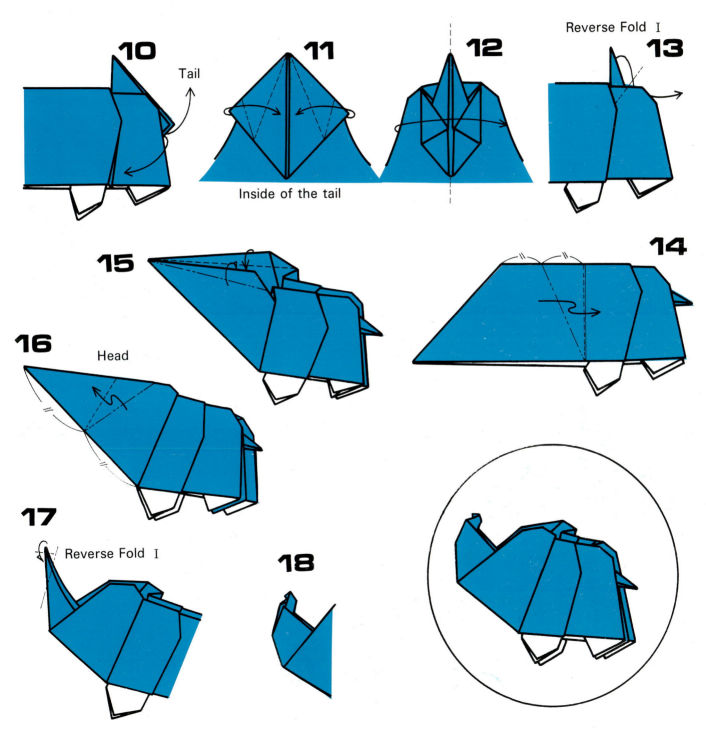

Fancy Case
(Container Ornament)

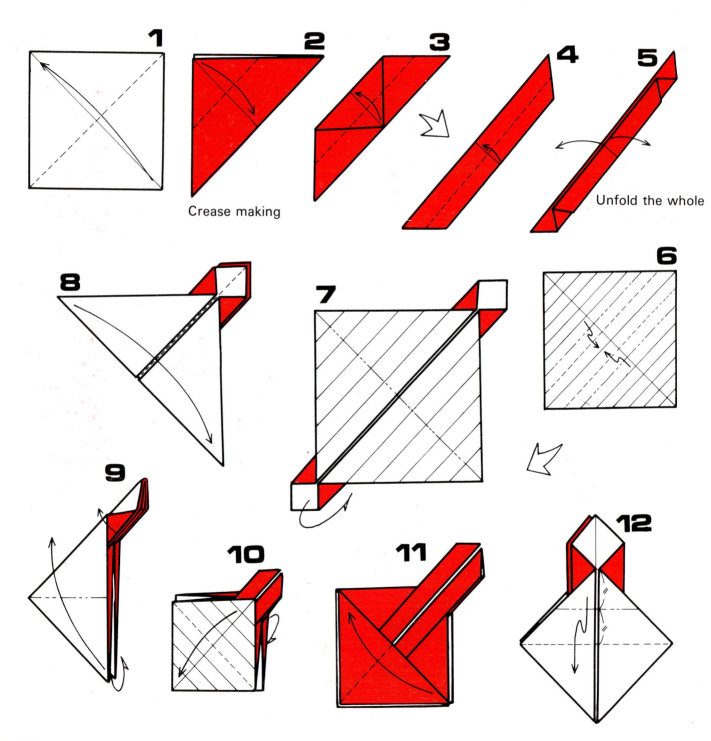

1

2
Crease making

3

4

5
Unfold the whole

6

7

8

9

10

11

12

12

13

14

15

16

Beak

20

19

18

17

DOGGIE

1

2

Make the bottom square flat

Open out the triangles to cover the whole
and make the head by Reverse Fold II

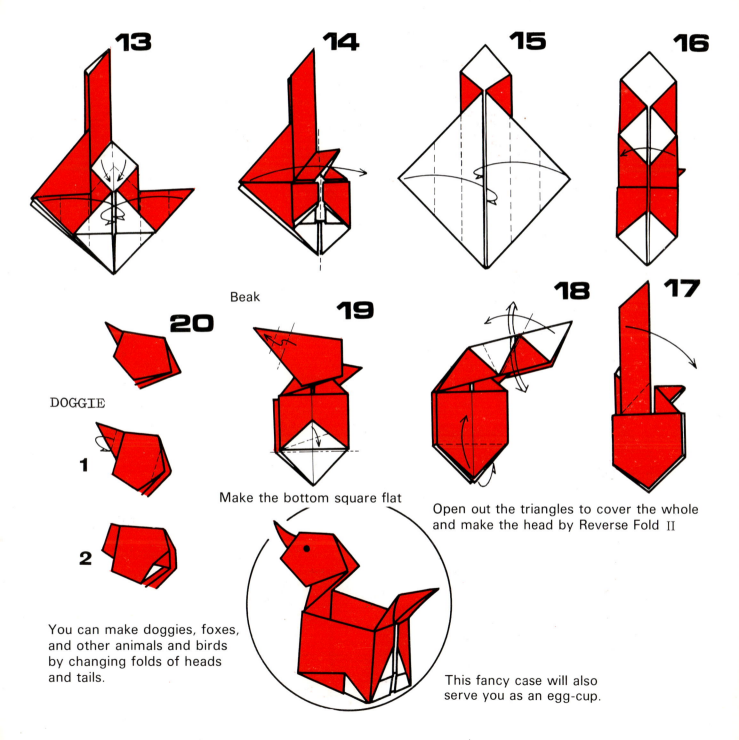

You can make doggies, foxes,
and other animals and birds
by changing folds of heads
and tails.

This fancy case will also
serve you as an egg-cup.

Frame

*Skip Step 5 if you can fold out the frame properly in Fig. 7—8, so that you may get rid of unnecessary creases when completed.

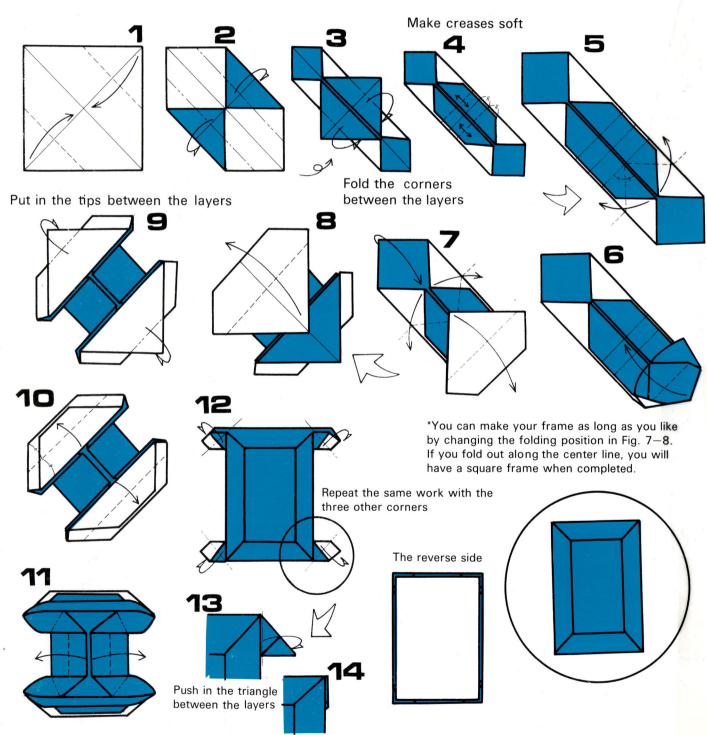

Make creases soft

1

2

3

4

5

Put in the tips between the layers

Fold the corners between the layers

9

8

7

6

10

12

*You can make your frame as long as you like by changing the folding position in Fig. 7—8. If you fold out along the center line, you will have a square frame when completed.

Repeat the same work with the three other corners

The reverse side

11

13

14

Push in the triangle between the layers

14

Paper Curtain
(Room Accessory)

Two sheets together with color outside

Two sheets make 1 piece and 2 folded pieces make 1 unit (A & B). So 4 sheets are used for 1 unit.

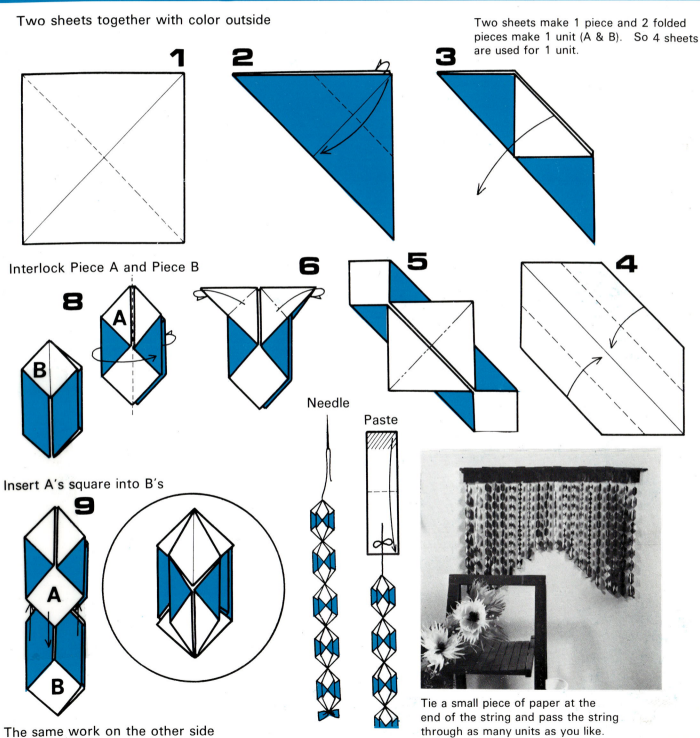

1

2

3

Interlock Piece A and Piece B

8

6

5

4

A

B

Insert A's square into B's

9

A

B

The same work on the other side

Needle

Paste

Tie a small piece of paper at the end of the string and pass the string through as many units as you like.

Coaster

COASTER 1

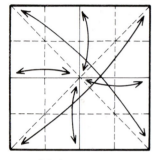

1 Make creases

2 Fold in along the creases

Make creases again and squash the triangles to squares

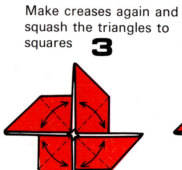

3

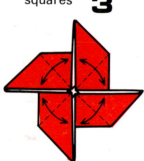

4

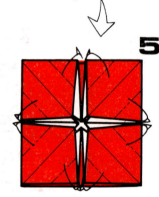

5

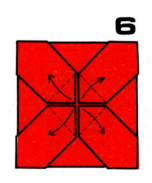

6

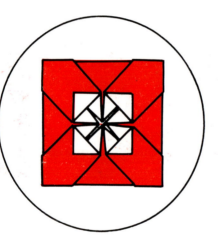

COASTER 2

1 Begin with Fig. 5 of COASTER 1

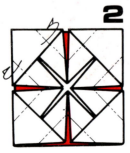

2

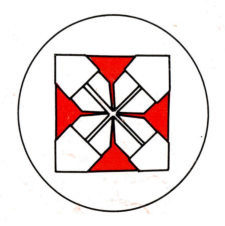

COASTER 3

1

Begin with Fig. 2 of COASTER 2

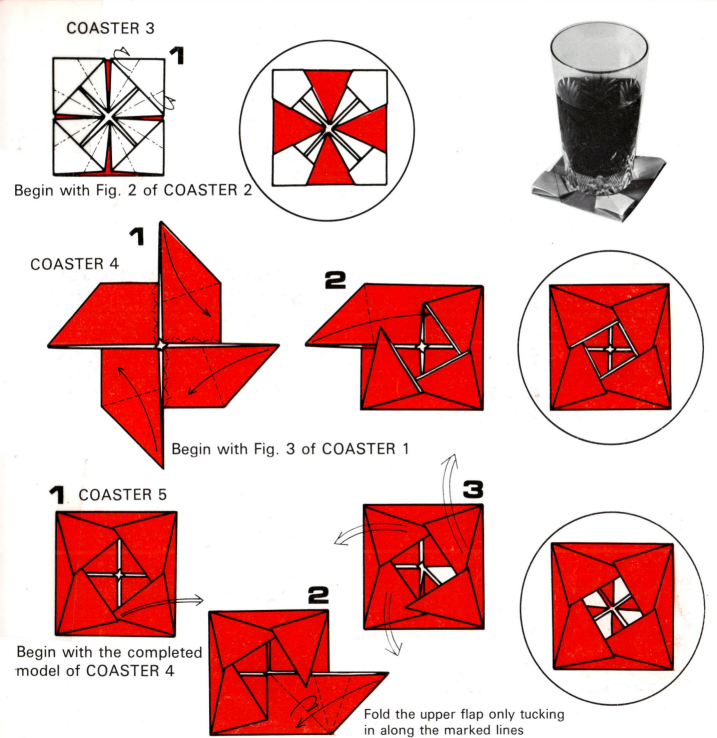

COASTER 4

1

2

Begin with Fig. 3 of COASTER 1

COASTER 5

1

Begin with the completed model of COASTER 4

2

3

Fold the upper flap only tucking in along the marked lines

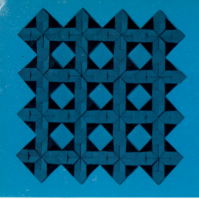

Tapestry & Table Center

Let us make a paper tapestry with Coaster 1 units

If you fold each unit with 2 pieces of different colors together with color outside, the completed work will be very pretty and colorful, like the one you find on the back cover.

1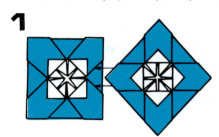

2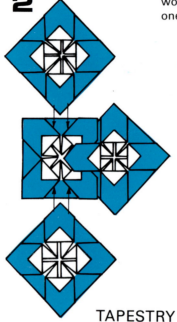

You can make the tapestry on the back cover by interlocking Coaster 3.

The reverse side

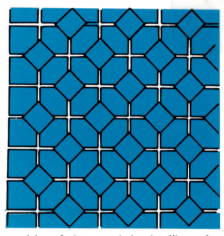

3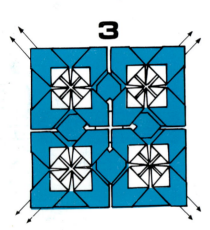

TAPESTRY

See how the other side of the work looks like when the units interlocked.

TABLE CENTER

Fold 16 units of Coaster 2 for a table center

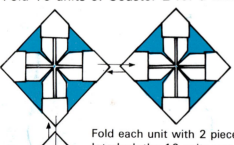

Fold each unit with 2 pieces of different colors. Interlock the 16 units one after another in such ways as shown here

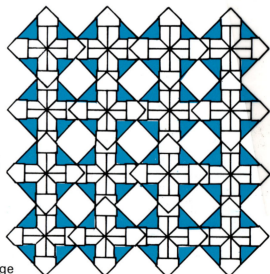

You can make your work as large as you like.

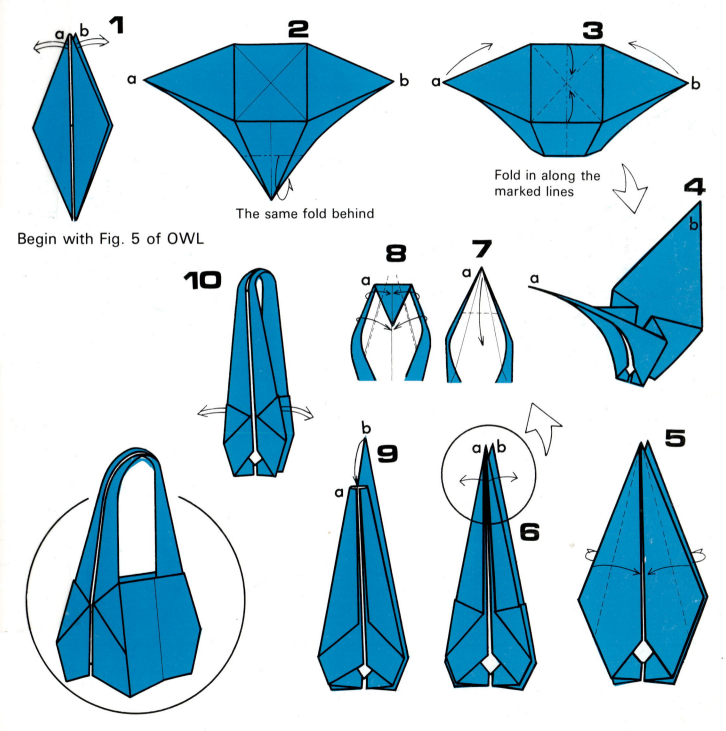

1 a b

Begin with Fig. 5 of OWL

2 a   b

The same fold behind

3 a   b

Fold in along the marked lines

4 b

a

5

6 a b

7 a

8 a

9 b

a

10

Fancy Flower

BLINTZ FOLD BASE

1

2

3

4

5

6

7

8

The same folding behind

9

10

The same folding with 3 other corners

11

Reverse Fold I

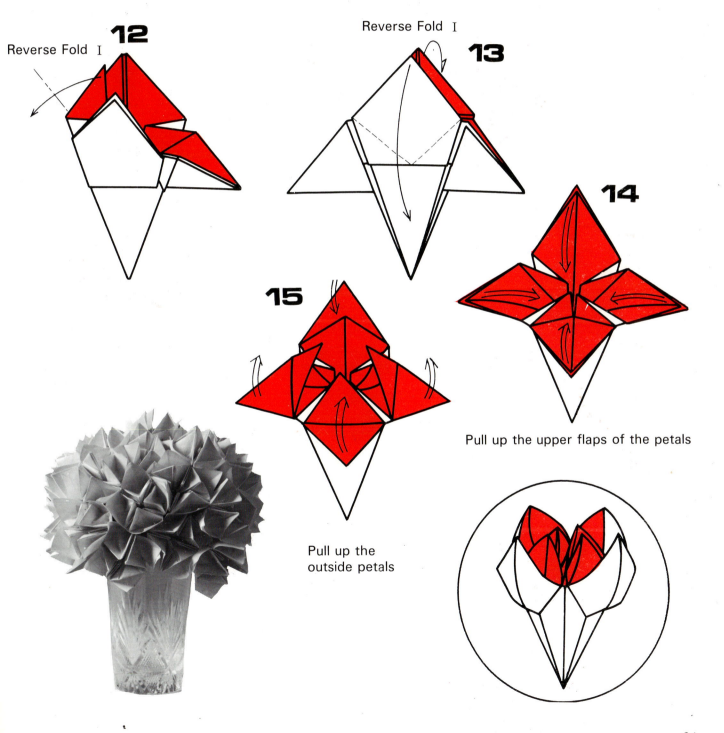

12

Reverse Fold I

Reverse Fold I

13

14

Pull up the upper flaps of the petals

15

Pull up the
outside petals

Vase

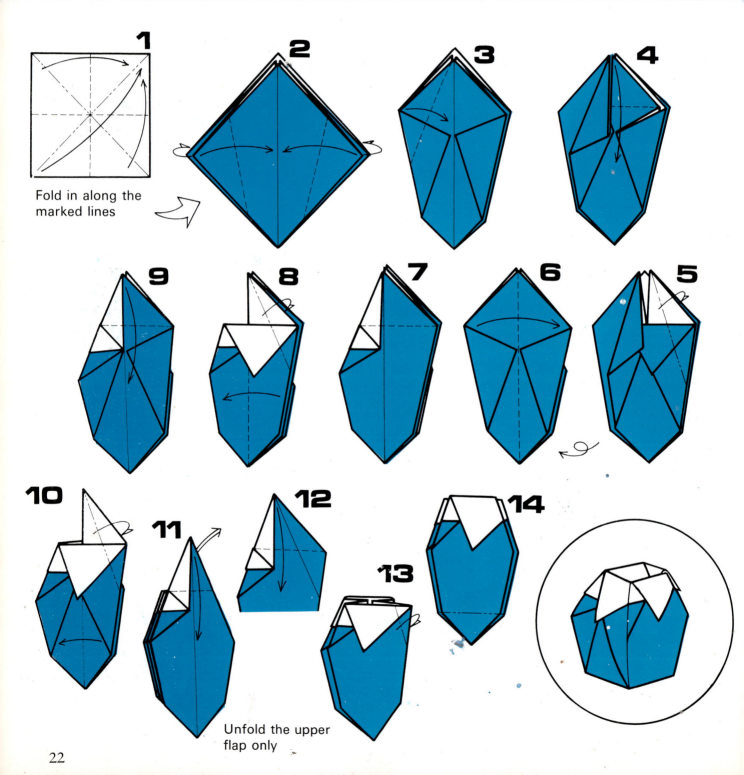

1

Fold in along the marked lines

2

3

4

9

8

7

6

5

10

11

12

13

14

Unfold the upper flap only

22

Hina Dolls
(Girls' Festival Dolls)

PRINCESS

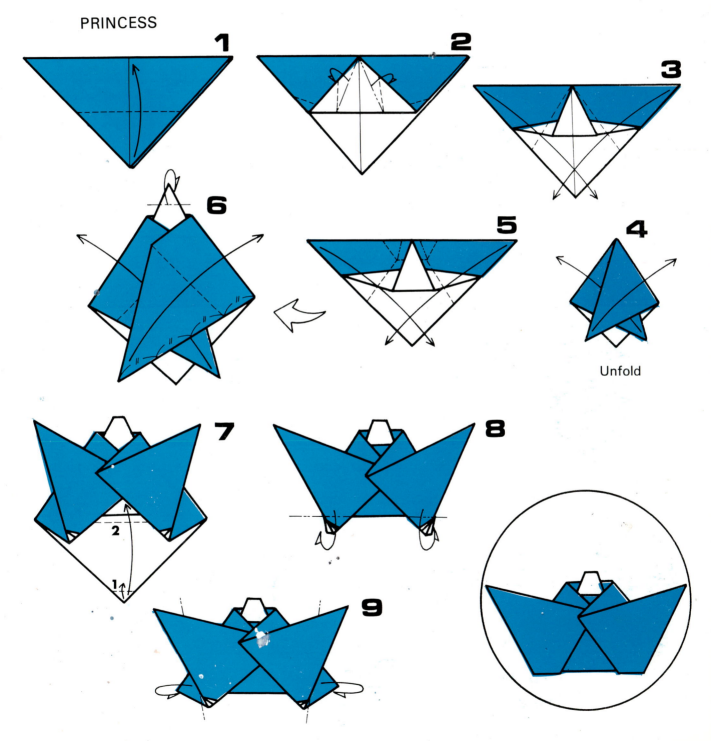

1

2

3

4

Unfold

5

6

7

2
1

8

9

PRINCE

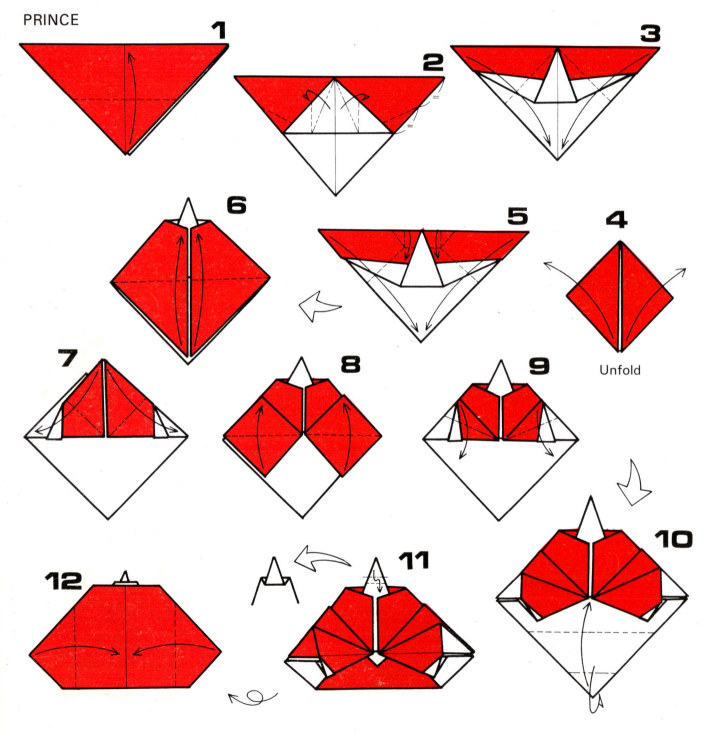

1

2

3

6

5

4

Unfold

7

8

9

10

11

12

24

The third of March is the Girls' Festival—Hina Matsuri in Japan. Children, especially girls, enjoy special treats and delicacies in front of the tier stand covered with a scarlet rug on which these royal couple, their followers, cute dolls and models of ancient furnishings as well as dishes and vehicles are displayed.

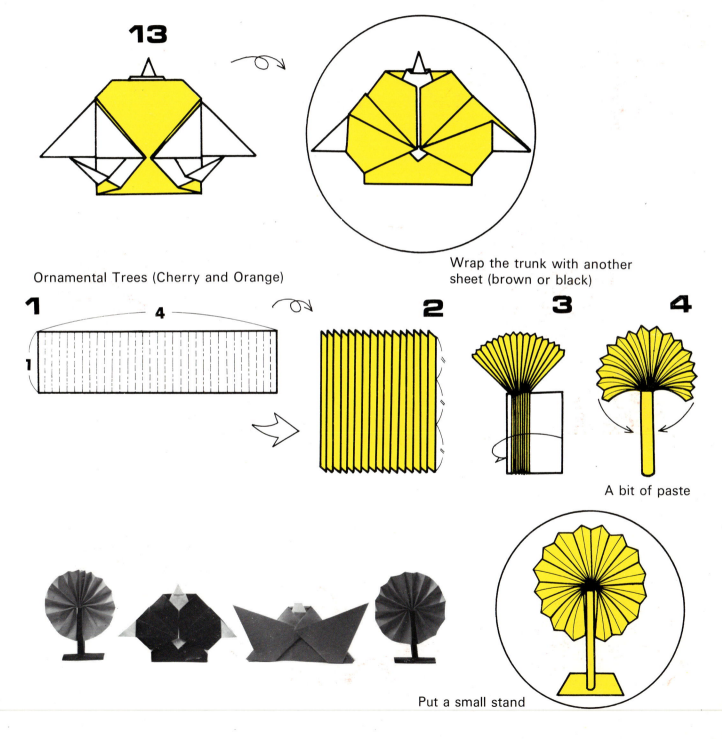

13

Wrap the trunk with another sheet (brown or black)

Ornamental Trees (Cherry and Orange)

1 4 1

2

3

4

A bit of paste

Put a small stand

Poinsettia

From the base of L. Montoya's Flower

How to make a hexagon from a square (1—3)

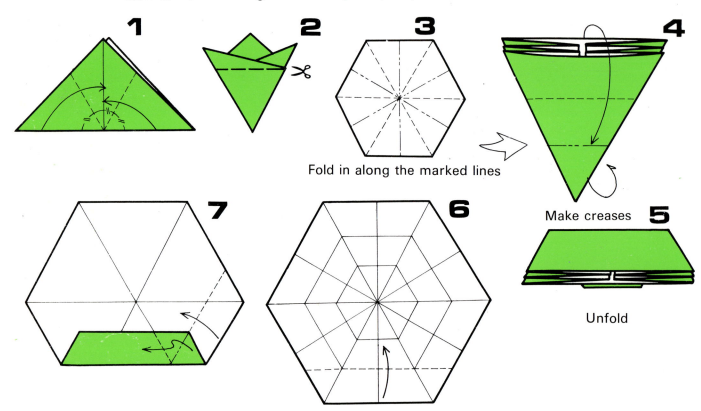

1

2 ✂

3

Fold in along the marked lines

4

Make creases **5**

Unfold

7

6

Repeat the same fold with the other corners

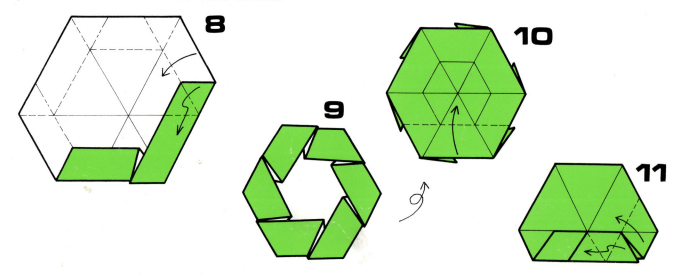

8

9

10

11

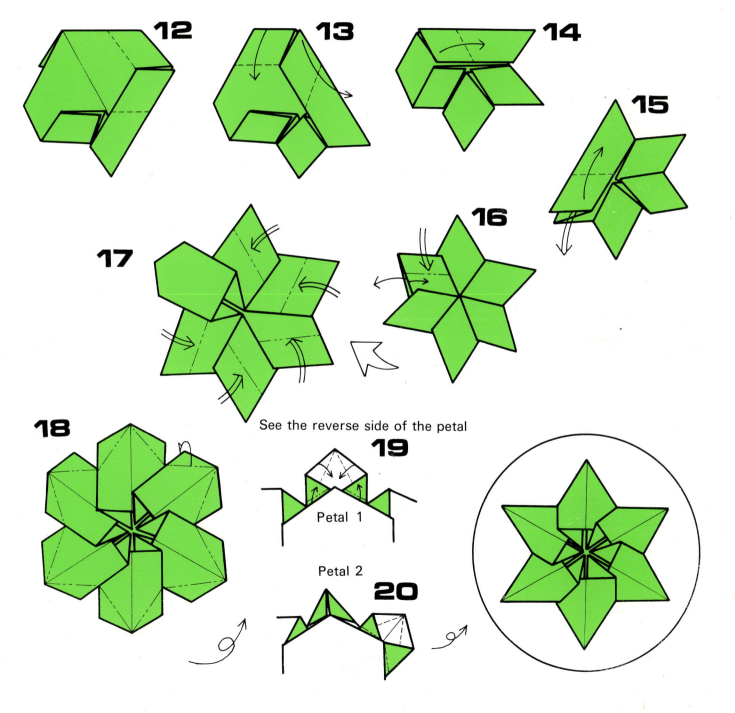

See the reverse side of the petal

Petal 1

Petal 2

Star (I)
(Christmas Tree Ornament)

STAR I   How to make a pentagon from a square (1—6)

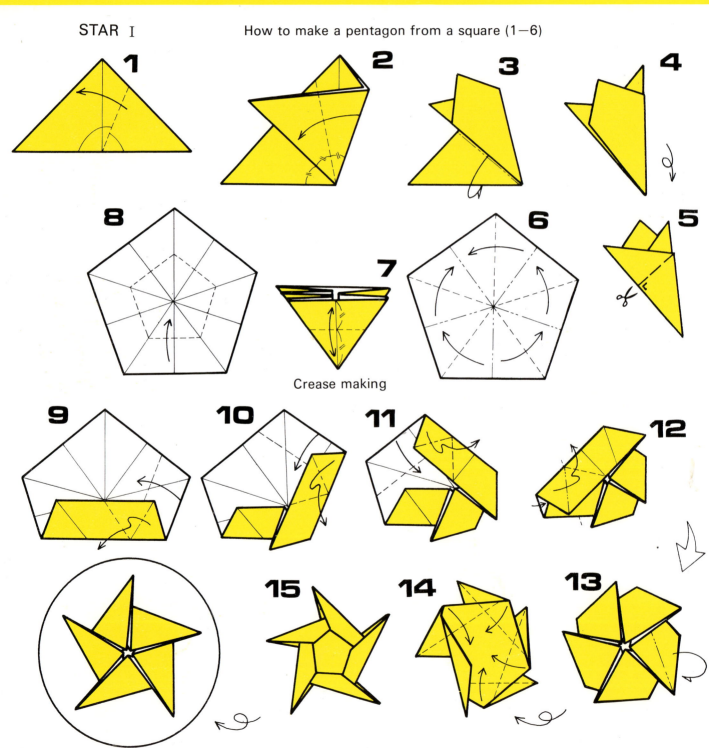

Crease making

28

Star (II)
(Christmas Tree Ornament)

STAR II

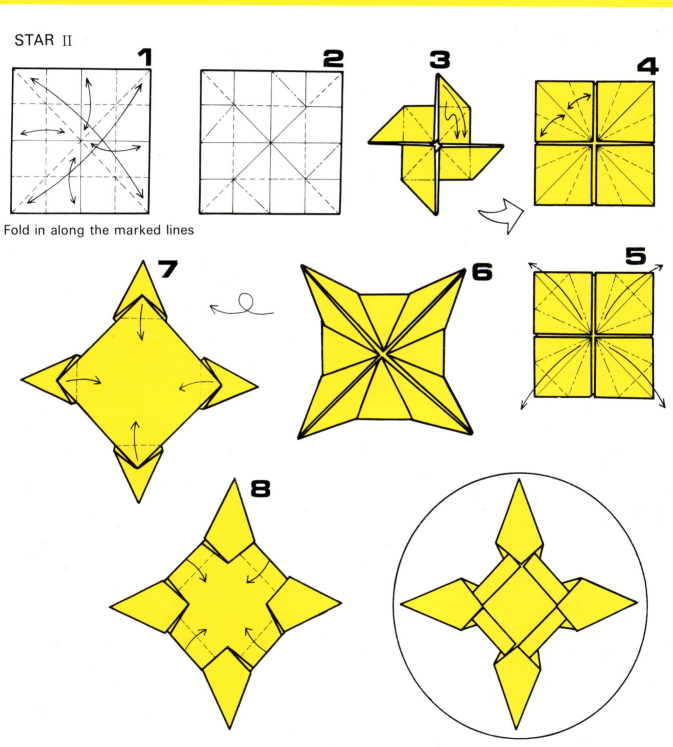

Fold in along the marked lines

Tree Ornament

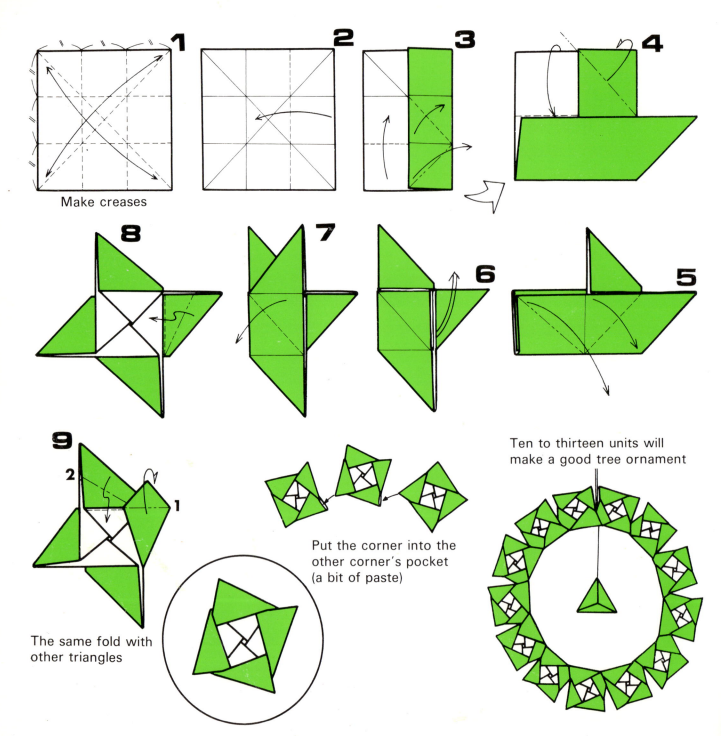

1 Make creases

2

3

4

5

6

7

8

9

2 **1**

The same fold with other triangles

Put the corner into the other corner's pocket (a bit of paste)

Ten to thirteen units will make a good tree ornament

30

Christmas Tree

You may put whatever you can fold on your Christmas tree.

THE FOLDINGS OF THE MODELS YOU HAVE LEARNED IN THIS BOOK

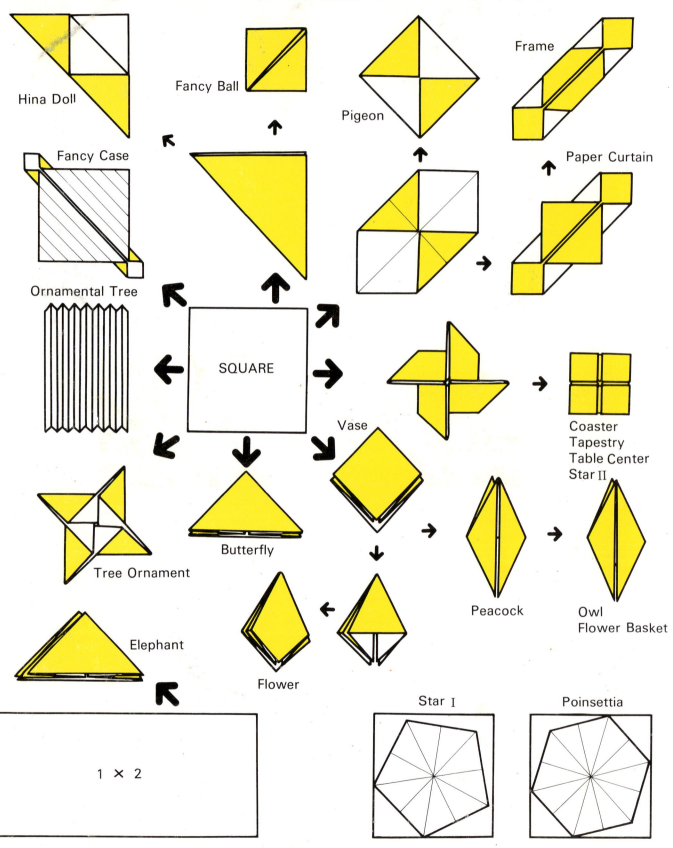

Hina Doll

Fancy Ball

Pigeon

Frame

Fancy Case

Paper Curtain

Ornamental Tree

SQUARE

Coaster
Tapestry
Table Center
Star II

Vase

Tree Ornament

Butterfly

Peacock

Owl
Flower Basket

Elephant

Flower

1 × 2

Star I

Poinsettia